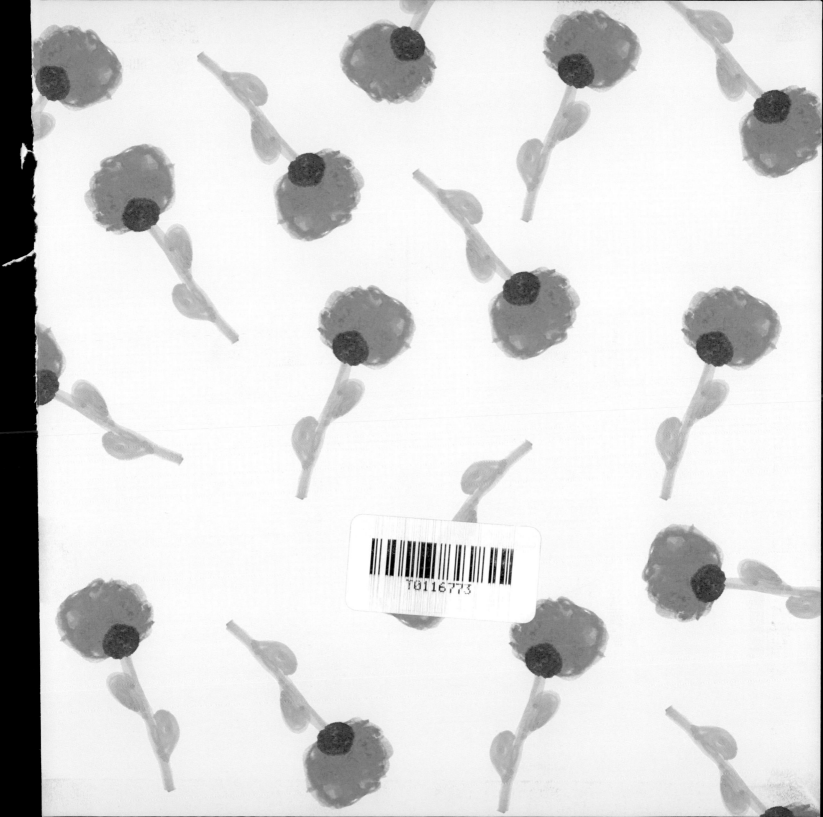

This book is given with love from

_____

to

_____

in honor of

_____,

who is shining down on you
from Heaven.

A Corner of Heaven

WRITTEN BY
Laura Dewire

ILLUSTRATED BY
Kailen Offutt

KiCam
PROJECTS

Printed in the United States of America

Book design by Mark Sullivan

ISBN 978-0-9970815-9-6

Published by KiCam Projects
www.KiCamProjects.com

For Kulen, Caleb, and Clare,

along with all other babies

in a special corner of Heaven.

There once lived
three little girls
who laughed a lot.

They played a lot.

They sang a lot.

They danced a lot.

And they loved a lot.

They lived with their mommy
and daddy in a cozy house
in a cozy town.

It was perfect.

One day their mommy and daddy, who adored each of them, told them some very exciting news. Soon, they would have another person to laugh with.

And play with.

And sing with.

And dance with.

And love.

"I hope he's smart," said the oldest daughter, who was wise and kind.

"I hope he's gentle," said the middle daughter, who was tender and mild.

"I hope he's funny," said the youngest daughter, who was silly and sweet.

And as this new baby grew,
the girls' dreams of him
grew bigger and bigger too.

What would he look like?

What would he talk like?

What would he *be* like?

After months and months
of waiting, the time came
for their baby brother
to be born.

Now, there's something you need to know about babies, and this is it: all babies are angels.

Sometimes angels have work to do on earth, and sometimes their work must be done in a special corner of Heaven.

21

And it was just so that this baby had a job to do that the Earth was too small to hold.

And it was very sad.

And for a time there was
no laughing.

And no playing.

And no singing.

And no dancing.

And it was very hard to love
in that dark time.

28

But even after the darkest nights, the sun will rise again.

And one day, just like that, the sun came out again—shining down from a corner of Heaven.

And the world was made beautiful and whole.

And the three sisters poured their love out and healed all that was broken.

Perhaps the most beautiful part about this baby is that if you ever want to see him, you need not look far...

For he is there,
shining down
on the three little girls
who laughed
a lot.

Laura Dewire is a dog-loving, coffee-drinking glitter fanatic from Wauwatosa, Wisconsin. She lives in Ohio, where she enjoys teaching her first- and second-graders at Saint Michael School and practicing yoga at her local library. She enjoys a red lip, a cold can of Diet Coke, a warm doughnut, and cooking in her cast-iron skillet. She tries with all her heart to live and love like Jesus every day.

Kailen Offutt likes her ponytails smooth and her crackers with cottage cheese. She'll do anything for strawberries, and she enjoys riding her bike and swimming on warm summer days. She has been known to break out into song at random times throughout the day. She loves her family, Jesus, school, and dancing.

Author's note

The first time I saw Kulen was in an illustration drawn by his sister, a student in my first-grade class. The assignment was to have each child create a portrait of his or her family. In the upper right-hand corner of Kailen's paper, a small baby was depicted with a figure who looked like Jesus. "This is my family," Kailen said. "Most of us live on Earth, but my baby brother, Kulen, lives in Heaven with God." It was both heartbreaking and touching to see that small angel in the corner of that paper.

It made me think about all the families affected by the loss of a child. One in four women will lose a child during pregnancy. Many times, as in Kulen's story, the child is lost to a family that already has other children. That got me thinking about the pain these parents must feel when tasked with sharing this tragic news with their other children. What if there were a book that could be used as a tool to help break the news? A book with pictures and language appropriate for young minds and hearts.

The tragic loss of a child to me is unthinkable, but it is my sincere wish that this book can be a beacon of hope for families—a shining light from a corner of Heaven.

Now I Lay Me Down to Sleep (NILMDTS) offers the gift of healing, hope, and honor to parents experiencing the death of a baby through the overwhelming power of remembrance portraits. Professional-level photographers volunteer their time to capture the only moments parents spend with their babies and gift the beautiful heirloom portraits free of charge. These priceless images serve as an important step in the healing recovery for bereaved families. NILMDTS remembrance photography validates the existence and presence of these precious babies by honoring their legacy. You can learn more about NILMDTS or find a photographer at www.nowilaymedowntosleep.org.

About the Offutts

Since Kulen was born into Heaven, the Offutt family has grown by one rainbow baby: Kowin Willow. The family resides in Brown County, Ohio, and enjoys family dinners, going to church, and spending time with family and friends. Their love for one another and love for the Lord are apparent to all who know them. Pictured (clockwise, from far left) are: Kamri-Beth, Teresa, Kowin, Andy, Karlie, Kailen, and Kulen.

. . . .

Lisa Hezlep is a Cincinnati-based photographer and a Now I Lay Me Down to Sleep volunteer photographer who created remembrance portraits for the Offutt family. She has remained close with the family and takes regular portraits of them, including the photos in this book. The blessing of Lisa's friendship is marked by the beautiful and selfless gift of her pictures. See more of Lisa's work at www.hezlepphotography.com.

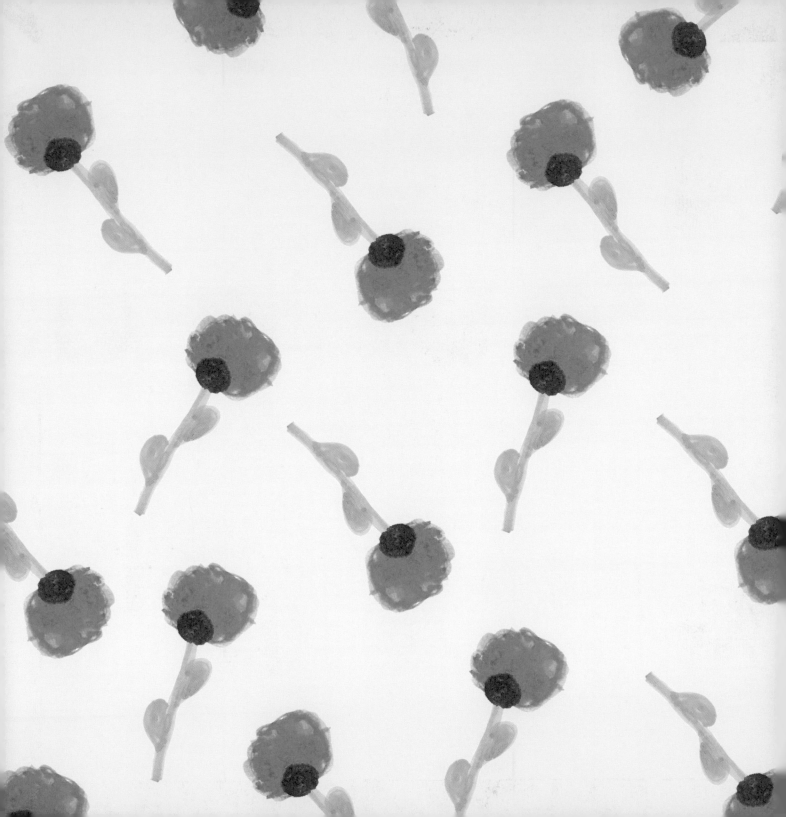